This is the heart-story of

....,

a woman who is made for

Romance, Adventure, and Beauty.

YOUR
Captivating
HEART
STASI ELDREDGE

**DISCOVER HOW
GOD'S TRUE LOVE
CAN FREE A
*Woman's Soul***

Published by
THOMAS NELSON
Since 1798

www.thomasnelson.com

Contents

{ 5 }

Foreword

By John Eldredge

I want you to do something really kind for your heart.

I want you to read this book.

Because your heart matters. (When was the last time anyone in your life told you that?). The life of a woman nowadays is full of demands, and deadlines, and a laundry basket overflowing with others people's needs and expectations. My guess is, it's been a long time since you've taken care of your heart as a woman.

But God is wooing you. That's why you picked up this book. God is calling to you to come away and take some time for your heart. Because it matters. It's true. Your heart matters. Your dreams, your hopes, your desires—they all matter and matter very much. God himself says so. He says, "Above all else, guard your heart, for it is the wellspring of life" within you (Proverbs 4:23).

We live in a time that is not very kind to the heart. The world is running at an absurd pace. The church is running at an absurd pace. By the time you get done trying to meet all the demands in your life, there is usually little or nothing at all left for yourself and your relationship with God.

But you can begin here. You can open your heart to the beautiful words and images in this book and let them carry you back to the love of God. Read it with your morning coffee. Or on your lunch breaks. Keep it with you in your purse and pull it out while you're waiting to pick up the kids. It will do you a world of good.

Think of it as a day at a spa for your heart—a gift from the One who loves you most.

I PRAISE YOU BECAUSE YOU MADE ME
IN AN AMAZING AND WONDERFUL WAY.
WHAT YOU HAVE DONE IS WONDERFUL.
I KNOW THIS VERY WELL.

PSALM 139:14

CHAPTER ONE

THE *Heart* OF A WOMAN

When I was a little girl, my favorite books were fairy tales. Snow White, Cinderella, Sleeping Beauty—you remember. I loved the stories, could have gazed at the beautiful pictures for hours. It's not that I thought my life *was* a fairy tale—far from it. Those fairy tales told me of a life I *wanted* to live. They awakened my heart to mystery and beauty, to danger and adventure, and above all, to romance and the happily ever after. I don't think I'm alone in this. *Only a fairy tale can awaken something set deep in the heart of every little girl.* Sometimes just the words *Once upon a time* could take me there.

Think of Snow White. It's the story of a lovely little girl who was every little girl. She was born with a song in her heart and a light in her soul that shone through her bright eyes. *She was meant for a world of beauty and wonder, of safety and protection.* She was supposed to be wanted. She was supposed to be enjoyed, delighted in, and encouraged. In this world where she was secure in love, she was meant to grow up into a beautiful, brave, and gifted woman. *But that wasn't the world she was born into.* Nor was I. Nor were you. Snow White gets lost in the forest. She eats the poison apple and falls into a deep slumber. O yes, the Prince comes, but only after suffering and betrayal. That is the part of the story we can't understand until we have grown up.

The Heart of a Woman

Many decades have passed since I was a little girl, and the heart that was stirred by those fairy tales now seems to have belonged to someone else. As for my adult life, I think I'd have to summarize my passage into womanhood as *busyness.* I got busy with the business of life. I worked hard and tried harder. I slept less, aimed higher, and failed more. At church, often I was exhorted to *do* more. Be more. Be better. Follow these seven steps, these six lifestyles, these twelve concepts. But in all of my trying, I didn't feel I was growing as a woman. *I just felt* tired. *Like Snow White, my heart fell into a deep slumber.*

I know I am not alone in this either. *As women we still long for intimacy and adventure; each of us longs to be the Beauty of some great story.*

But the desires set
deep in our hearts
seem like a luxury—
granted only to those
women who get their acts
together. The message to the rest of us—whether from a
driven culture or a driven church—is *try harder*. So we bury
our hearts and try to get on with life.

And that is not a wise thing to do, for as the scriptures tell
us, the heart is central. *"Above all else, guard your
heart, for it is the wellspring of life"* (**PROVERBS 4:23**).
Above all else. Why? Because God knows that our heart is
core to who we are. Your heart as a woman is the most
important thing about you.

Think about it: God created you *as a woman*. "God created
man in his own image . . . male and female he created
them" (**GENESIS 1:27**). Whatever it means to bear God's

image, you do so *as a woman.* Your feminine heart has been created with the greatest of all possible dignities—as a reflection of God's own heart. *You are a woman to your soul, to the very core of your being.* And so the journey to discover what God meant when he created woman in his image—when he created you as his woman—that journey begins with your heart.

Another way of saying this is that *the journey begins with desire.*

Look at the games that little girls play, and if you can, remember what you dreamed of as a little girl. Look at the movies women love. Listen to your own heart and the hearts of the women you know. What is it that a woman wants? What does she dream of? *Every woman in her heart of hearts longs for three things: to be romanced, to play an irreplaceable role in a great adventure, and to unveil beauty.* That's what makes a woman come alive. That's what the fairy tales were trying to tell us.

Romanced

Do you know what the bestselling kind of novel is? Historical fiction? No. Mystery? No. Crime dramas? Nope. The fiction books outselling all others, by millions, are romance novels. And I'm not talking about great writing here. These are the novels with the buxom woman on the cover, usually standing on a cliff, her clothes suggestively disheveled, the wind whipping her hair. Who can be buying them? Women are buying them.

We are buying them. Their authors have tapped into something core to the heart of women—our desire to be wooed and won, to be pursued and fought for, to be *romanced*.

Some of us are embarrassed by this desire. We diminish it, mock it, downplay it. And when the desire has gotten us into trouble and caused us pain, we do our best to kill it. *Yet our desire for romance refuses to die*. Oh it may be buried, or hidden deep within, but it remains. And a good thing, too. For we don't have to be embarrassed by our desire to be romanced. It is a true, glorious longing in our hearts! It is, in fact, where we bear the image of God. *God* loves *romance!* He created it. He invented sunsets and roses and music and love. He says, "You will seek me and find me when you seek me with all your heart!" (JEREMIAH 29:13).

God wants to be pursued. So do we.

Now, being romanced isn't all that a woman wants, and I am certainly not saying that a woman ought to find the meaning of her existence in whether she is being or has been romanced by a man or not. *But don't you see that you want this?* To be desired, to be pursued by someone who loves you, to be a priority to someone? Most of our addictions as women flare up when we feel that we are not loved or sought after. At some core place, maybe deep within, every woman wants to be seen, delighted in, and pursued. We long to be *romanced*.

Irreplaceable Role

We also want to be essential, needed, irreplaceable! A woman doesn't come alive being merely useful. See, there is something fierce in the heart of a woman. Simply insult her children, her man, or her best friend and you'll get a taste of it. *A woman is a warrior too.* But she is meant to be a warrior in a uniquely feminine way. Sometime before the sorrows of life did their best to kill the desire in us, most young women wanted to be part of something grand, something important. Before doubt and accusation take hold, most little girls sense that they have a vital role to play; they want to believe there is something in them that is needed and needed desperately.

Isn't this true of God? He wants to be needed. He wants to play an irreplaceable role in our lives. He wants to live in a shared adventure with us. This is the whole story of the Bible. And here, too, in your heart, you have a heart like God's. *Women love adventures of all sorts.*

Whether we crave the adventure of riding horses (most girls go through a horse stage), whitewater rafting, going to a foreign country, performing on stage, having children, starting a business, or diving ever more deeply into the heart of God, we were made to be a part of a great adventure. An adventure that is *shared*.

Sometimes the idea of living as a hermit appeals to all of us. No demands, no needs, no pain, no disappointments. But that is because we have been hurt or worn out. In our heart of hearts, that place where we are most *ourselves*, we don't want to run away for very long. *Our lives were meant to be lived with others.* Made in the image of perfect relationship, we are relational to our core and filled with a desire for transcendent purpose. We long to be part—an *irreplaceable* part—of a shared adventure.

Beauty to Unveil

Finally, there is Beauty. Think of the stories you love, the movies that you watch over and over again. *Pride and Prejudice. The Lord of the Rings. Sleepless in Seattle. Little Women. The Sound of Music.* And then think of who you want to be in those stories. *You want to be the Beauty of the story, don't you?* The woman who not only attracts the good man but who, with her golden heart, also captures all those around her and inspires them to life. The woman who is beautiful inside and out.

This is why little girls play dress up. Little boys play dress up, too, but in different ways. Our sons were cowboys for years. Or army men. Jedi knights. But they never once dressed up as bridegrooms, fairies, or butterflies. Little boys do not paint their toenails. They don't dress up in

Mommy's jewelry and high heels. They don't sit for hours and brush each other's hair. *Boys want to be the brave Prince; we want to be Snow White.*

Remember twirling skirts? Most little girls go through a season where they will not wear anything if it does not twirl (and if it sparkles, so much the better). Hours and hours of play result from giving little girls a box filled with hats, scarves, necklaces, clothes. Plastic beads are priceless jewels; hand-me-down pumps are glass slippers. Grandma's nightie a ballroom gown. Once dressed, they dance around the house or preen in front of a mirror. *Little girls' young hearts intuitively want to know they are lovely.* Some will ask with words, "Am I lovely?" Others simply ask with their eyes. Verbal or not, whether wearing a shimmery dress or covered in mud, all little girls want to know.

Think of your wedding day—or the wedding day you dream of having. How important is your dress as a bride? Would you just grab the first thing in your closet, throw on any old thing? A friend of ours is getting married in six

months, and this young woman
has seen her share of boys and
heartbreaks. Her tale of
beauty has many hurts
to it. But as she told
us about trying on
wedding dresses and
finding just the right one, the
weariness faded away and she was radiant.
"I felt like a princess!" Isn't that what you
dreamed of? It is a timeless yearning.

Now, we know that the desire to be beautiful
has caused many women untold grief. (How
many diets have you been on?) Countless tears
have been shed and hearts broken in its pursuit. Beauty has
been extolled and worshipped and kept just out of reach for
most of us. For others, beauty has been shamed, used, and
abused. Many women have learned that possessing beauty
can be dangerous. And yet, and this is just astounding,

in spite *of all the pain and distress that beauty has caused us as women, our desire for it remains.*

And it's *not* just the desire for an outward beauty, but more; it's a desire to be captivating in the depths of *who we are. Cinderella is beautiful, yes, but she is also* good. Her outward beauty would be hollow were it not for the beauty of her heart. That's why we love her.

Ruth may have been a lovely, strong woman, but she attracts Boaz with her unrelenting courage, vulnerability, and faith in God. Esther is the most beautiful woman in the land, but her bravery and her cunning good heart are what move the king to spare her people. This isn't just about dresses and makeup. For now, don't you recognize that a woman yearns to be *seen* and to be thought of as captivating? *We desire to possess a beauty that is worth pursuing, worth fighting for, a beauty that is core to who we truly are.*

An Invitation

The desires God placed in your heart were put there for a reason. They reveal the secret of who you really are and the life you *are* meant to live. God didn't place these desires in your heart to torment you. No. *God placed these desires in your heart to guide you and draw you into discovering the woman he made you to be, and the life he created you to live.*

> *Delight yourself in the LORD,*
> *and he will give you the desires of your heart.*
> PSALM 37:4

Only when the Prince comes and kisses Snow White awake does she come to herself. She not only awakens, she also rides off into the sunset with her beloved where no more evil will ever befall her. This is what we need as well. *We need our Prince, who is Jesus, to kiss us awake through healing and through love.* And this, my friends, is exactly what he offers to do. "I have loved you with an everlasting love," he says (JEREMIAH 31:3). "You have stolen my heart, my sister, my bride; you have stolen my heart with one glance of your eyes" (SONGS 4:9).

I have some wonderful news for you: *Fairy tales are* true. The reason we loved them as little girls (and still do now, if we're completely honest) is that they speak to the secret written on our hearts; they reveal the true story we were created for. But in order to find that life we once dreamed of, *we need to be kissed awake again. We need to see.*

Beauty and the Beast

It's that time of the month again, *and although, yes, I would like to be the Beauty of the story, currently*

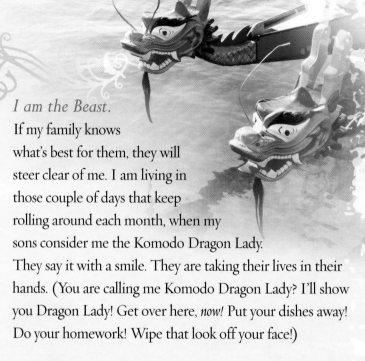

I am the Beast.
If my family knows
what's best for them, they will
steer clear of me. I am living in
those couple of days that keep
rolling around each month, when my
sons consider me the Komodo Dragon Lady.
They say it with a smile. They are taking their lives in their
hands. (You are calling me Komodo Dragon Lady? I'll show
you Dragon Lady! Get over here, *now!* Put your dishes away!
Do your homework! Wipe that look off your face!)

I ask you—is it too much to ask that people drive the
speed limit? And do people even *know* where the turn
signal is in their cars? If you eat the last granola bar out
of the box, how difficult is it, really, to throw the box away?
Yes, my hormones are raging. Yes, I am feeling everything a bit
more heightened than the other twenty-eight days in

the month. But that doesn't mean that what I am feeling isn't true.

Too often I have diminished my emotions, my sadness, my rage by blaming it on my ever-changing hormones rather than taking my self, my heart, all of me to God and asking for his eyes and his help. *See, the Beast is alive in this Beauty. And like the Beast in the classic fairy tale, I need to be transformed.* Lucky for me, lucky for all of us, that is exactly what Jesus came to do. And exactly what happens when my soul finds its rest in the love of God.

I don't want to be the Beast. I want to be the Beauty. I don't even like being around *myself* when I am feeling so negative. That is not who I long to be. *When I am raging, I lose all hope of becoming the woman I truly want to be.* Like you, I have desires in my heart. Some so fragile that exposing them to the weight of air may be too much for them. I am keenly aware of my longings for God. I ache with the desire to play my irreplaceable role in a heroic, shared adventure where I offer my strength and my beauty for the goodness of all. I want to *know* at all times that I am delighted in. But I don't.

I am reminded of Pascal's metaphor that says our unmet longings and unrequited desires are in fact "the miseries of a dethroned monarch." They bear witness to the truth of this fairy tale. *All people are like kings or queens in exile who cannot be happy until they have recovered their true state.* What would you expect the Queen of a kingdom and the Beauty of the realm to feel when she wakes to find herself a laundress in a foreign land? *A woman's struggle with her sense of worth points to something glorious she was* designed *to be.* The great emptiness we feel points to the great place we *were created* for. It's true. All those legends and fairy tales of the undiscovered Princess and the Beauty hidden as a maid are more accurate than we thought. There's a *reason* we resonate with them so deeply.

And the reason is found in the story of our creation.

The Creation Story

The story is found in Genesis chapters 1-3. (You might want to read it again). My husband, John, described this beautifully in our book *Captivating*, which I highly recommend that you read. When you remember the story, you'll note that *there is a progression to creation*. What begins as formless and void slowly takes shape. God is the Master Artist and he begins his creation with broad brushstrokes—light and dark, land and sea, heaven and earth.

Then God adds intricacy and detail as he continues his work. After he creates the oceans and gives them their borders, he fills them with creatures of stunning variety. Dolphins. Puffer fish. Whales! After he creates the land, he then brings forth the trees and the birds nesting in them. As he continues his work, he moves from fish and birds to animals. Yes, a trout is an amazing creature, but how much more so is a horse!

Then something truly astonishing takes place. *God sets his own image on the earth.* He creates a being like himself. He creates a son.

> *The LORD God formed the man from the dust of the ground and breathed into his nostrils the breath of life, and the man became a living being.*
>
> **GENESIS 2:7**

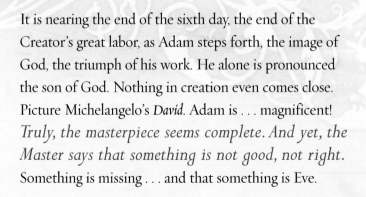

It is nearing the end of the sixth day, the end of the Creator's great labor, as Adam steps forth, the image of God, the triumph of his work. He alone is pronounced the son of God. Nothing in creation even comes close. Picture Michelangelo's *David*. Adam is . . . magnificent! *Truly, the masterpiece seems complete. And yet, the Master says that something is not good, not right.* Something is missing . . . and that something is Eve.

*And the Lord God cast a deep slumber on the human, and he
slept, and He took one of his ribs and closed over the flesh where
it had been, and the Lord God built the rib He had taken from
the human into a woman and He brought her to the human.*

GENESIS 2:21-22, ALTER

*Eve is the crescendo, the final, astonishing work of
God.* Woman. In one final flourish, creation comes to a
finish not with Adam, but with Eve. She is the Master's
finishing touch. Imagine with me now some painting or
sculpture that captures this, like the stunning Greek
sculpture of the goddess Nike of Samothrace, the winged
beauty, just alighting on the prow of a great ship, her
beautiful form revealed through the thin veils that sweep
around her. *Eve is . . . breathtaking!*

What does Eve Speak to Us?

The story of Eve holds such rich treasures for us to discover.
The essence and purpose of a woman are unveiled here in the
story of our creation. *We women bear the image of God.*

But in a way that only the feminine can speak. God wanted to reveal something about himself, so he gave us Eve. What can we learn from her?

First, we discover that God is relational to his core, that he has a heart for romance. Second, he longs to share adventures with us—adventures we cannot accomplish without him. And finally, God has a beauty to unveil. A beauty that is captivating and powerfully redemptive. *Romance, adventure, and beauty— just like in the fairy tales.*

Romance and Relationships

The vast desire and capacity a woman has for intimate relationships tells us of God's own vast desire and capacity for intimate relationships. In fact, this may be *the* most important thing we ever learn about God—that he yearns for relationship with us. "Now this is eternal life; that they may know you, the only true God" (JOHN 17:3). *The whole story of the Bible is a love story between God and his people.* He yearns for us. He *cares.* He has a tender heart.

> *I will give them a heart to know me, that I am the Lord. They will be my people, and I will be their God, for they will return to me with all their heart.*
> JEREMIAH 24:7

What a comfort to know that this universe we live in is relational at its core, that *our God is a tenderhearted*

God who yearns for relationship with us. If you have any doubt about that, simply look at the message he sent us in Woman. Amazing! Not only does God long *for us*, but he longs to be loved *by* us.

Can there be any doubt that God wants to be sought after? The first and greatest of all commands is to love him (DEUTERONOMY 6:5; MATTHEW 22:36-37; MARK 12:29-30). *God* wants *us to love him.* To seek him wholeheartedly.

A woman longs to be sought after too. *God longs to be* desired. *Just as a woman longs to be desired.* This is not some weakness or insecurity on the part of a woman, that deep yearning to be desired. God feels the same way. Remember the story of Martha and Mary? Mary chose God, and Jesus said that is what he wanted. "Mary has chosen what is better"—*she chose me* (LUKE 10:42).

Life changes dramatically when romance comes into our lives. Christianity changes dramatically when we discover that it, too, is a great romance. That God yearns to share a life of beauty, intimacy, and adventure with us. Eve—God's message to the world in feminine form—invites us to romance. This whole world was made for romance—the rivers and the glens, the meadows and beaches. Flowers. Music. Kisses. But we have a way of forgetting all that, losing ourselves in work and worry. *God—through Eve—makes romance a priority of the universe.*

O yes, our God has a passionate, romantic heart. Just look at Eve.

An Adventure to Share

While Eve has a glory for relationship, she also is essential for much more. Back in Genesis, when God sets his image bearers on the earth, he gives them their mission:

> And God said, "Let us make a human in our image, by our likeness, to hold sway over the fish of the sea and the fowl of the heavens and the cattle and the wild beasts and all the crawling things that crawl upon the earth.

And God created the human in his image,
in the image of God He created him,
male and female He created them.
And God blessed them, and God said to them, "Be fruitful and
multiply and fill the earth and conquer it, and hold sway over
the fish of the sea and the fowl of the heavens and every beast
that crawls upon the earth."

GENESIS 1:26-28 ALTER

Call it the Human Mission—to be all and do all God sent us here to do. And notice—the mission to be fruitful and conquer and hold sway is given *both* to Adam *and* to Eve. "And God said to *them . . .*" (v. 28). Eve is standing right there when God gives the world over to us. She has a vital role to play; she is a partner in this great adventure. *Everything that human beings were intended to do here on earth—all the creativity and exploration, all the battle and rescue and nurture—we were intended to do* together. In fact, not only is Eve needed, she is *desperately* needed.

{ 35 }

That longing in the heart of a woman to share life together as a great adventure—that comes straight from the heart of God, who also longs for this. He does not want to be an option in our lives. He does not want to be an appendage, a tagalong. Neither does any woman.

God is essential. In his image, Eve is also. She has an irreplaceable role to play. And so women are endowed with fierce devotion, an ability to suffer great hardships, a vision to make the world a better place.

You see, *women have been essential to every great move of God.* Yes, Moses led the Israelites out of Egypt but only after his mother risked her life to save him! Closer to our time, Clara Barton was instrumental in starting the Red Cross. Harriet Beecher Stowe's *Uncle Tom's Cabin* put fire into people's hearts to end slavery in the United States. Rosa Parks kicked the Civil Rights movement into gear with her quiet act of courage. Eunice Kennedy Shriver created the Special Olympics. Mother Teresa inspired the world by bringing love to countless thought unlovable. And millions of other women quietly change the world every day by bringing the love of God to those around them.

Beauty to Unveil

Beauty is essential to God. That is to say, *beauty is the essence of God.*

In *Wild at Heart*, my husband, John, wrote,

> The reason a woman wants a beauty to unveil, the reason she asks, *Do you delight in me?* is simply that God does as well. God is captivating beauty. As David prays, "One thing I ask of the Lord, this is what I seek . . . that I may . . . gaze upon the beauty of the LORD" (**PSALM 27:4**). Can there be any doubt that God wants to be *worshipped?* That he wants to be seen, and for us to be captivated by what we see?

But in order to make the matter perfectly clear, God has given us Eve. The crowning touch of creation. *Beauty is the essence of a woman.* I want to be perfectly clear that I mean *both* a physical beauty and a soulful/spiritual beauty. The one depends upon and flows out of the other. Yes, the world cheapens and prostitutes beauty, making it all about a perfect figure few women can attain. But Christians minimize beauty, too, or over-spiritualize it, making it all about "character." We must recover the prize of beauty. The church must take it back. Beauty is too vital to lose.

God gave Eve a beautiful form and *a beautiful spirit.* She expresses beauty in both. Better, she expresses beauty simply in who she is. Like God, beauty is her *essence.*

Beauty Speaks

And what does beauty say to us? Think of what it is like to be caught in traffic for over an hour. Horns blaring, people shouting obscenities. Exhaust pours in your windows, suffocates you. Then remember what it's like to come into a beautiful place, a garden or a meadow or a quiet beach. *Amid beauty, there is room for your soul.* It expands. You can breathe again. You can rest. It is good. All is well. I sit outside on a summer evening and just listen and behold and drink it all in. My heart begins to quiet, and peace begins to come into my soul. "All will be well," as Julian of Norwich concluded, "and all manner of things will be well."

That is what beauty says: All will be well.

And this is what its like to be with a woman at rest, a woman comfortable in her feminine beauty. She is enjoyable to be with. She is lovely. In her presence our hearts stop holding their breath. We relax and believe once again that all will be well. And this is also why a woman who is striving is so disturbing, for a woman who is not at rest in her heart says to the world, "All is not well. Things are not going to turn out all right." Instead a striving woman is "like a fountain troubled," as Shakespeare said, "muddy, ill-seeming, thick, bereft of beauty." *We* need *what beauty speaks.* What it says is difficult to put into words. But part of beauty's message is . . . *all is well. All will be well.*

Whatever else it means to be a woman, *femininity is depth and mystery and complexity, with beauty as the very essence.*

Now, lest despair set in, let me say as clearly as I can:

Every woman has a beauty to unveil.

Every woman.

Because she bears the image of God. She doesn't have to conjure it, go get it from a salon, have plastic surgery, or get her teeth capped. No. *Beauty is an essence that is given to every woman at her creation.*

STASI ELDREDGE

Created for Beauty

I take great encouragement that the Beast is transformed in the tales and that the Beauty often is first found scrubbing the floors or hidden in the cellar. Yes, we are created for beauty, to be the Beauty in the story. Yes, like the heroine in every fairy tale, we have been wronged, assaulted. *We are not what we were meant to be. But like every great tale, that is not the end of the story.* Oh no. God intended us to carry his image to the world as women, through our feminine hearts, as women who are glorious, fierce, strong, tender, and beautiful. That is the heart Jesus has come to restore.

The best of all news is that Christianity is a gospel of restoration. *Jesus isn't scrapping your heart; instead, he wants to restore it to you.* For it is *in* your heart that you bear his image and *from* your heart that the life you were meant to live flows.

CHAPTER TWO

DAMSELS IN *Distress*

*W*hen I was five years old, my family went to visit my father's parents in New Jersey. His parents were a very "proper" family. We were required to sit up straight at their dining table. It was the sort of house where you could only speak when spoken to and even then in quiet, respectful tones. And I, in my girlish exuberance, stood in the middle of their living room, on *top* of their coffee table and belted out every song in my five-year-old repertoire. I wasn't only offering my grandparents a taste of my true self, *I was asking them a Question* about *my true self.*

You see, every little girl is asking one fundamental Question, a question that is core to her heart. Little boys have a core Question too. Little boys want to know, Do I have what it takes? All that rough and tumble, all that daring and superhero dress-up, all of that is a boy seeking to prove that he does have what it takes. He was made in the image of a warrior God. Nearly all a man does is fueled by his search for this validation, this longing that comes from his heart's deepest Question.

Little girls, on the other hand, want to know, Am I lovely? Do you see me? Am I worth fighting for? The twirling skirts, the dress-up, the longing to be pretty and to be seen—all of that is about seeking an answer to our Question. When I was standing on top of the coffee table singing my heart out, I wanted to capture attention—especially my father's attention. *I wanted to be captivating. We all did.* And even as adults, nearly all a woman does now is fueled by her search for an answer to her Question. Because life has not gone the way it was supposed to go. Not for any of us. Remember Snow White?

The End of the Innocence

Evil befell her. Snow White's young life was introduced to envy, jealousy, and rage. She was subjected to blows to her body and to her heart . . . from the very people who were supposed to cherish and safeguard her. At an age much too young, her world shattered and she knew she was no longer safe. *To protect her very life, her heart went into exile.*

The story of Snow White is the story of every woman. Oh, the details vary, the circumstances differ, but the theme is the same. It is a mythic tale for our lives.

No longer safe at home, the little girl (who was a true princess, by the way) was driven away and wandered the woods alone and afraid. Her life had been spared by the kind woodsman, but how was she to live? Fate in the form of gentle animals helped her, and Snow White found a place for herself in the home of the seven dwarves.

There her heart began to flourish again. She sang as she worked. She enjoyed the beauty around her. She danced again! *Hope was revived.* And while she was busy about what felt like an ordinary life, a wicked witch came to her in disguise and offered her poison.

In the form of a beautiful apple, *Snow White didn't recognize the poison for what it was* any more than she recognized the poor beggar woman as the sorceress who wanted her dead. (Wanted her *heart* destroyed, cut out, and brought to her in a box!) Snow White ate the apple, ingested the poison, and fell prey to its effects.

We also fall prey to poison. All the time. We take it in because we don't recognize it for what it truly is. If only it came from the hand of a stooped beggar woman offering us an apple! But no, it's not that obvious. To us these days, the poison enters our bodies, our hearts, in the form of sentences. Words spoken to us from those we love and those we don't. Accusatory sentences that began when we were very young. Names we were called that told us who we really were as women and who we will never be. We all know that the children's taunt "sticks and stones may break my bones but words will never hurt me" is a lie. Bones can heal. *Evil words spoken to us can fester in our hearts,* doing untold damage to our lives.

Sometimes the poison enters our hearts from an event, a betrayal, an assault. But it is what we come to believe about ourselves that can kill. Like Snow White, a part of us dies, falls into a deep slumber, seems to "go away."

The Fall of Woman

When God created Eve she was endowed with qualities that speak of God. Eve is inviting. She is vulnerable. She is tender. She embodies mercy. She is also fierce and fiercely devoted. *Eve is given to the world as the incarnation of a beautiful, captivating God*—a life offering, lifesaving lover.

Is that how you experience the women in your life? Is that how people experience you?

Something has happened. *Something has separated us from the life of our hearts we knew as little girls.* Something has separated us from the life we long for as women. You remember . . . A garden. A snake.

The fruit taken and eaten from the forbidden tree. Genesis 3 happened. We fell.

The story goes like this.

> Now the serpent was the shrewdest of all the creatures the Lord God had made. "Really?" he asked the woman. "Did God really say you must not eat of any of the fruit in the garden?"
>
> "Of course we may eat it," the woman told him. "It's only the fruit from the tree at the center of the garden that we are not allowed to eat. God says we must not eat it or even touch it, or we will die."
>
> "You won't die!" the serpent hissed. "God knows that your eyes will be opened when you eat it. You will become just like God, knowing everything, both good and evil."
>
> The woman was convinced.
>
> GENESIS 3:1–6 NLT

The woman was *convinced*? That's it? How long did it take? And what was she convinced of?

Eve was convinced that God was holding out on her.
She was convinced that he did not have her best interest at
heart. She was convinced that in order to have the best
possible life, she must take matters into her own hands
and so, reaching out, she does. She ate some of the fruit
and gave some to her husband to eat as well. And paradise
was lost. We lost the garden. We lost the beauty of the
world. We lost unblemished relationship with God.

And we have been reaching ever since . . . trying to make our
lives work out as best they can on our own terms. You see,
the lies the snake hissed to Eve in the garden are the
very same lies the snake whispers to us in the middle of
the night and in every vulnerable moment of our lives. We,
too, are tempted to believe that God does not have our best
interests in mind, for if he did, then we wouldn't feel so
alone, we wouldn't have the sorrows that we bear, we wouldn't
still be waiting for our dreams to come true.

In every fiber that makes up the fabric of our faith *we are*
tempted to doubt God rather than believe that his

heart is good, that his heart is for us. Because the sorrows are real. The loneliness and the heartbreak and the pain are all very real. So, what is a woman to do? Well, what do we tend to do?

When a woman falls from grace, as all women have done, what is most deeply marred is her tender vulnerability— *beauty that invites to Life.* She becomes a dominating, controlling woman—or, on the other end of the spectrum, a desolate, needy, mousy woman. Or some odd combination of both, depending on the story of her life.

Controlling Women

Think of all the wicked women in fairy tales—the step-mothers and stepsisters and the witches and bad queens. They are all, every one of them, controlling women. *Fallen Eve controls her relationships. She refuses to be vulnerable.* And if she cannot secure her relationships,

{ 53 }

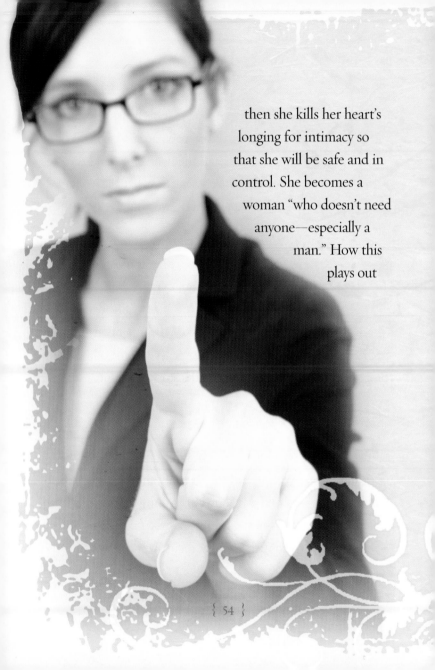

then she kills her heart's longing for intimacy so that she will be safe and in control. She becomes a woman "who doesn't need anyone—especially a man." How this plays out over the course of her life and how the wounds of her childhood shape her heart's convictions are often a complex story, one worth knowing. But beneath it all is a simple truth: *Women dominate and control because they fear their vulnerability.* They refuse to trust their God.

Now, this is not to say a woman can't be strong. What I am saying is that far too many women forfeit their femininity in order to feel safe and in control. Their strength feels more masculine than feminine. There is nothing inviting or alluring, nothing tender or merciful about them. Snow White's own stepmother cannot stand the goodness and vulnerability and beauty of Snow White. She sends a woodsman to kill her and bring her heart back in a box.

Desolate Women

If on the one side of the spectrum we find that Fallen Eve becomes hard, rigid, controlling, then on the other side we find women who are desolate, needy, far *too* vulnerable. Desolate women are ruled by the aching abyss within

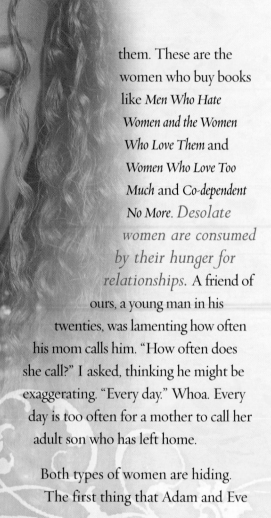

them. These are the women who buy books like *Men Who Hate Women and the Women Who Love Them* and *Women Who Love Too Much* and *Co-dependent No More*. *Desolate women are consumed by their hunger for relationships.* A friend of ours, a young man in his twenties, was lamenting how often his mom calls him. "How often does she call?" I asked, thinking he might be exaggerating. "Every day." Whoa. Every day is too often for a mother to call her adult son who has left home.

Both types of women are hiding. The first thing that Adam and Eve do after they sin and fall from grace is hide. "I was afraid because I was naked; so I hid" (GENESIS 3:10). *We hide because we are afraid.*

You see underneath all our controlling and striving, manipulating and indulging, hiding and shrinking back, there is fear. *Fear that we will be found out, that the answer to our Question is a resounding* no. Fear that once we are found out, those around us will run for the hills and we will end up abandoned and alone.

What we need to see is that *all our controlling and all our hiding actually serve to separate us from our hearts.* We lose touch with those longings that we knew when we were young, those core desires that make us women.

And down in the depths of our hearts, our Question—*Am I lovely? Do you see me? Do you want to see? Am I worth fighting for?*—remains unanswered. Or it remains answered in the way it was answered so badly in our youth. When we were young, we knew nothing about Eve and what she did and how it affected us all. As girls, we did not know to bring our heart's Question to God, and before we learned to do so, most of us were given answers in a very painful way. *We have been wounded into believing awful things about ourselves.* And so every woman comes into the world set up for a terrible heartbreak.

Wounded

Beneath every striving, controlling, indulging, hiding, or desolate woman is a wounded little girl.

You see, none of us gets a pain-free life. Not even the women whose life and appearance look so perfect . . . from a distance. *To be alive means that we are and have been wounded.* Longfellow said, *"If we could see into the secret lives of even our enemies, we would find enough suffering and sorrow there to end all hostilities."*

A pain-free life is a fantasy. And you don't live in a fantasy. Instead, your life is much more like the stuff of fairy tales. *In fairy tales, damsels are in distress* and grandmothers fall prey to big bad wolves. Children are lost and endangered, and little girls wander the woods alone and afraid, wondering if their prince will ever come.

Fairy tales have villains. There are the wicked witches, the evil stepmothers, and the fierce dragons. Our story has a villain, too. The story of your life, of every woman's life, is the story of the long and sustained assault upon your

heart by *the enemy who knows what you could be and who fears you.*

This is not Eden. Not even close. We are not living in the world our hearts were made for. Although all of our stories are different, *all of us were wounded and none of us had a perfect childhood.* Adam fell, as did Eve, and most of our fathers and mothers continued the sad story. They were not perfect and most of them carried unhealed wounds of their own. They did not provide the things our hearts needed in order to become lovely, vulnerable, strong, adventurous women.

Wounded Hearts

The wounds that we received as young girls did not come alone. They brought *messages* with them, messages that struck at the core of our hearts, right in the place of our Question. *As children, we didn't have the faculties to process and sort through what was happening to us.* Our parents were godlike. We believed them to be right. If we were overwhelmed or belittled or hurt or abused, we believed that somehow it was because of us—the problem was with us.

Many women still feel that, by the way. We can't put words to it, but down deep we fear there is something terribly wrong with us. We think, *If I were a princess, then my prince would have come. If I were the daughter of a King, he would have fought for me. We can't help but believe that if we were different, if we were better, then we would have been loved as we so longed to be.*

Our Stories

Sandy's father abused her, and her mother turned away. It wrought great evil upon Sandy's soul. This taught Sandy two basic things about femininity:

> *To be a woman is powerless—vulnerability has nothing good about it; it's just "weak."*

> *To be feminine is to draw unwanted intimacy to yourself.*

Does it surprise you that she doesn't want to be feminine? Like so many sexually abused women, *she finds herself longing for intimacy* (she was created for that) but fearing to look the least bit alluring to a man. She's settled for "competent and efficient professional woman," kind but guarded, never too attractive and never, ever in need, never "weak."

Some women who were sexually abused choose another path. Or, perhaps more honestly, *they find themselves compulsively looking for love.* Although they never received love through the sexual abuse, they did experience some sort of intimacy, and now they give themselves over to one man after another, hoping to somehow heal the wrongful sexual encounters with sex that has love to it.

Melissa's mother was a wicked woman who beat her children with a split two-by-four board about fifteen inches long. "I was absolutely terrified of my mother," Melissa confessed. "She seemed psychotic and would play evil mind games. Most of the time we never really knew why we were getting beat. My father did nothing. One thing I did know is that with every blow my hatred for her deepened. She turned my sister into a fragile mush of a person, and I vowed she would never do that to me. *I vowed that I would be tough, hard, like a rock.*" This she became, well into her adult life.

An Unholy Alliance

Over the years we've come to see that the only thing *more* tragic than the things that have happened to us is what our hearts have done with those things.

Words were said, painful words. Things were done, awful things. And our wounds shaped us. Something inside of us *shifted. We embraced the messages of our wounds.* We accepted a wrong view of ourselves, and that view influenced how we chose to relate to our world. We made a vow never to be in that place again. We adopted strategies to protect ourselves from being hurt again. *A woman who is living out of a broken, wounded heart is a woman who is living a self-protective life.* She may not be aware of it, but it is true. It's our way of trying to "save ourselves."

We also developed ways of trying to get something of the love our hearts crave. *The ache is there.* Our desperate need for love and affirmation. Our thirst for some taste of romance, adventure, and an important role to play. So we turned to boys or to food or to romance novels; we lost ourselves in our work or at church or in some sort of service.

All this adds up to the women we are today. Much of what each woman calls her "personality" is actually the mosaic of her choices for self-protection plus her plan to get something of the love she was created to enjoy.

The problem is *our plans have nothing to do with God.*

The wounds we received and the messages they brought form a sort of unholy alliance with our fallen nature as women. *From Eve we received a deep mistrust of the heart of God towards us.* Clearly, he's holding out on us. We'll just have to arrange for the life we want. We will control our world. But there is also an ache deep within, an ache for intimacy and for life. We'll have to find a way to fill it. A way that does not require us to trust anyone, especially God. A way that will not require vulnerability.

True Love is Our Hope

God sees it all. He sees our sin. He sees our wounds and the ways we have mishandled our hearts. He sees our lack of trust in him and our longing to trust him more. He is well-acquainted with our fallen nature. And amid all our messiness *God says to us,* You are lovely. Do not hide your face from me. Come to me. I love you. Let me heal you. So the woman in the Song of Songs, who in some way is every woman, is able to say, "Dark am I, yet lovely" (1:5). She knows she is loved.

We can know it too.

Dear heart, there is hope. Whether or not you feel it. It is there as surely as the sunrise. *There is hope. There is healing. There is* life. For you. For me. For all of us. This tale is about to take a wonderful turn.

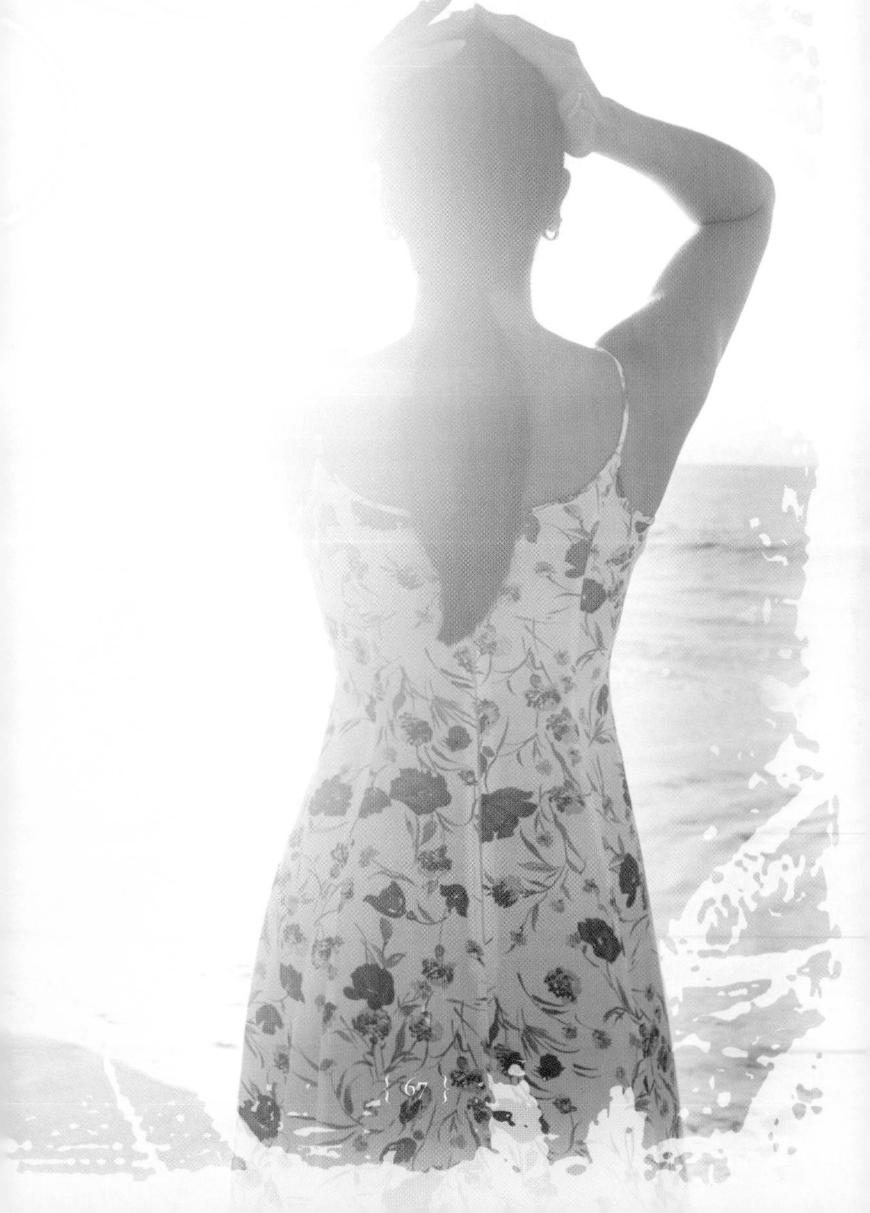

CHAPTER THREE

BELOVED
Daughter

*S*arah was sixteen years old and the adventure of the day beckoned her to come, enjoy, explore! She was supposed to go to school, but Sarah spent the day in the rugged and stunning mountains instead. *It had been a glorious day.* Driving home in the early evening Sarah's thoughts wandered. She felt so at home in the mountains, so refreshed. Suddenly, a car flashed into Sarah's view as it ran a red light and struck her car head on.

The force of the impact sent Sarah, who was not wearing a seat belt, crashing headfirst through the windshield. As she flew through the air, her left knee caught on the hood ornament of her car. She hit the ornament with such power that it ripped into her leg, caught her, and then thrust her back through the broken glass into the smashed front seat of her car.

Badly hurt and bleeding profusely, Sarah's stunned mind took a while to kick into gear. Her first thoughts were, *I deserved this. If I hadn't skipped school, this never would have happened. Wounded and bleeding, she believed it was her fault.*

Does that sound familiar?

Yes, Sarah made a few bad choices. But even so, the accident was in no way her fault. Nor was it a punishment from God. *Some of our bad choices do have consequences.* If we don't study for the test, we won't get a good grade no matter how hard we pray for help while we're taking it. If we never say no to our children, and if we don't discipline them with good boundaries, they will grow into self-centered people who feel entitled to receive whatever they want. They will not grow into adults who "rise up and call [us] blessed" (Proverbs 31:28).

There are ramifications to how we choose to live. *But every wound that has come our way has* not *been what we deserved* nor was it always the result of our choices!

As fate would have it, Sarah's next-door neighbor was in the car behind her and witnessed the whole accident. Using her cell phone, she called Sarah's parents as they were getting ready for dinner. "You'd better come down here. Sarah's been in an accident," she said to Sarah's father. The neighbor's calmness led Sarah's dad to imagine a mere fender bender, and so with irritation and no rush, he drove to the intersection to help with the insurance paperwork.

The situation he had anticipated was not the one he arrived to find.

When Sarah's father pulled up to the intersection, he found police cars, fire trucks, and ambulances. He saw the smashed car of the other driver . . . and he saw his daughter's car, utterly demolished. Walking toward it with fear, he could see Sarah in the front seat. Sarah could see him as well and she began to yell out, *"Daddy, it's not my fault! Daddy, it's not my fault!"*

"I can *see* that!" he assured. What he could also see were the firefighters trying to use the Jaws of Life to remove the door from car so they could extricate Sarah from the tangled metal, but the hydraulic tools weren't working. Precious minutes passed. The Jaws of Life were literally not cutting it.

So Sarah's father took action. *With fierce passion and love for his daughter,* he pushed the firefighters aside, and with his bare hands he ripped the door from the car.

True story.

In that moment, *Sarah's father forever answered her question of whether or not she was loved by him.* Did he delight in her? Would he protect her, fight for her? *Was she worth it?* Yes, yes *and forever* yes!

And here is some wonderful news: *Your* true, heavenly Father also has forever answered the question of whether or not *you* are worth fighting for, worth pursuing. Are you loved? "For God so loved the world that He gave His only begotten Son, that whoever believes in Him should not perish but have everlasting life" (JOHN 3:16 NKJV). Did it cost him to love? It cost him everything. And he says, you are worth it.

> *Behold what manner of love the Father has bestowed on us, that we should be called children of God!*
>
> 1 JOHN 3:1 NKJV

Are you loved? Look at the cross. Look at the Father who sent his Son for you. *For you.*

I don't have a story like Sarah's that helps me to know that my earthly father loved me. But *I do have the story of a Heavenly Father who is my True Father.* He has adopted me into his family because like you, he had me in mind before the foundation of the earth (Ephesians 1:4).

Knowing the love of the Father—*our* Father—resting in it, lavishing in it, trusting in it, begins to bring the healing that we so desperately need. All of us, to one extent or another, are wounded and bleeding. *All of us need to know once and for all if we are loved now.* In this moment. And not just when we get our act together, lose the twenty pounds, get the promotion, the degree, the ring. And your Father, your True Father wants you to know.

We must ask Him.

Receive His Love

Then he went with Sara into her little sitting room and they bade each other good-bye. Sara sat on his knee

and held the lapels of his coat in her small hands, and looked long and hard at his face.

"Are you learning me by heart, little Sara?" he said, stroking her hair.

"No," she answered. *"I know you by heart. You are inside my heart."* And they put their arms round each other and kissed as if they would never let each other go.

Frances Hodgson Burnett's timeless classic *A Little Princess* touches something core in the heart of every little girl— and every woman. Every little girl was made to live in a world with a father who loves her unconditionally. From her earthly dad, every girl first learns who God is, what he is like, and how he feels about her. God is "Our Father which art in Heaven" (MATTHEW 6:9 KJV). He means initially to reveal himself to his daughters and his sons through the love of our dads. *We were meant to know a father's love, be kept safe in it, be protected by it, and blossom within it.*

But I never called my own father "Daddy." "Papa" was what fathers were called in movies. Many of us grew up in homes where the correct term for Dad was "Sir." For me, it was impossible to experience intimacy with and dependence upon a father who was emotionally absent and rarely home. My dad didn't want to know me. I was a disappointment to him.

I have come to see that *I viewed my Heavenly Father through the lenses of my experiences of my own father.* And for me, that meant my Heavenly Father was distant, aloof, unavailable, hard to please, easily disappointed, quick to anger, and often hard to predict. True, I wanted to please him. But because, to me, God the Father was difficult to fathom and not especially inviting, my relationship with God centered on my relationship with his Son. *Jesus liked me. I wasn't so sure about his Dad.*

Years into my Christian life, *I began to hunger to know God more deeply as my Father.* I asked him to reveal himself to me as my Dad. In answer, God invited me to take a journey into my deep heart that took surprising turns and continues still. First, God led me into taking a much closer look at my own father. Who was he really? How did he really feel about me? What did I even remember? *God invited me to go with him into the deep places of my heart* that were hidden and wounded and bleeding still from heartbreaks and wounds I had received from my father. Places I did not want to go. Memories I did not want to revisit. Emotions I did not want to feel. The only reason I said yes to God, that I would travel there, was because I knew he would go with me. He would hold my heart.

A core part of our heart was made for Daddy. Made for his strong and tender love. That part is still there, still longing. Open it to Jesus and to your Father God. Ask him to come and love you there. Meet you there. We've all tried so hard to find the fulfillment of this love in other people, and it never, ever works. Let us give this treasure back to the One who can love us best.

Father, I need your love. Come to the core of my heart. Come and bring your love for me. Help me to know you as the True Father you really are. Reveal yourself to me. Reveal your love for me. Come, and father me.

Why He Came

Let the truth saturate your heart that it was because of his *deep, unconditional love* for you that God the *Father* sent his only Son so that whoever believes in him will not perish but have everlasting life! Yes, *it was* for you that the King of kings orchestrated the most daring raid of the universe. It was for you that the Ancient of Days sneaked into the enemy camp disguised as a baby. *It was because of his great love* for you that Jesus endured death on a cross, scorning its shame. You *are the joy that was set before him* (Hebrews 12:2).

I lived many years of my Christian life in good churches, churches that taught me the place of worship and sacrifice, faith and suffering, and gave me a love for the Word of God. But in all those years the central ministry of Jesus was never explained to me. I understood, as most Christians do, that Christ came to ransom us from sin and death, to pay the price for our transgressions through his blood shed on the cross, so that we might be forgiven, might come home to the Father.

It's true! It's so wonderfully true. Only . . . *there is* more!

The purposes of Jesus Christ are not finished when one of his precious ones is forgiven. Not at all. Would a good father feel satisfied when his daughter is rescued from a car accident, but left in ICU? Doesn't he want her to be healed as well? In the same way, *God has much more in mind for us.* Listen to this passage from Isaiah 61:1-3. (It might help to read it very slowly, carefully, out loud to yourself.)

> The Spirit of the Sovereign LORD is upon me,
> because the LORD has anointed me
> to preach good news to the poor.
> He has sent me to bind up the brokenhearted,
> to proclaim freedom for the captives
> and release from darkness for the prisoners,

to proclaim the year of the LORD's favor
and the day of vengeance of our God,
to comfort all who mourn,
and provide for those who grieve in Zion—
to bestow on them a crown of beauty
instead of ashes,
the oil of gladness
instead of mourning,
and a garment of praise
instead of a spirit of despair.

This is the passage that Jesus pointed to when he began his ministry here on earth. Of all the Scriptures he could have chosen, this is the one he picked on the day he first publicly announced his mission (see Luke 4:14–21).

It must be important to him. It must be central. What does it mean? It's supposed to be really good news, that's clear. It has something to do with healing hearts, setting someone free. Let me restate it in words more familiar to us.

> *God has sent me on a mission.*
> *I have some great news for you.*
> *God has sent me to restore and release something.*
> *And that something is you.*
> *I am here to give you back your heart and set you free.*
> *I am furious at the Enemy who did this to you, and I will fight against him.*

Let me comfort you.
For, dear one, I will bestow beauty upon you
where you have known only devastation.
Joy, in the places of your deep sorrow.
And I will wrap your heart in thankful praise
in exchange for your resignation and despair.

Now that is an offer worth considering. What if it were true? I mean, *what if Jesus really could and would do this for your broken heart,* your wounded feminine soul? Read it again, and ask him, *Jesus—is this true for me? Would you do this for me?*

He can, and he will . . . if you'll let him.

You are the glorious Image Bearer of the Lord Jesus Christ. You have been assaulted. You have fallen to your own resources. Your Enemy has seized upon your wounds and your sins to pin your heart down. Now the Son of God has come to ransom you, *and* to heal your broken, wounded, bleeding heart, *and* to set you free from bondage. He came for the brokenhearted captives. That's me. That's you. *He came to restore the glorious creation that you are. And then set you free . . . to be yourself.*

> The LORD their God will save them on that day
> as the flock of his people.
> They will sparkle in his land
> like jewels in a crown.
> How attractive and beautiful they will be!
>
> ZECHARIAH 9:16–17

The healing of your feminine heart is available. *The restoration we long for is central to Jesus' mission,* central to the purposes of your True Father.

There simply isn't enough room in this little book to explore more deeply the path to healing that is available for us. Let me once again refer you to the book I wrote with John, *Captivating: Unveiling the Mystery of a Woman's Soul.* Outlined in the book are steps to healing and even suggested prayers to help you on your way. Not as once-in-a-lifetime prayers—but as a way to live. It is the path that I and so many are on, and *the fruit is substantial healing and truly beautiful.*

Ask Him to Answer Your Question

Those of you who have read *The Little Princess* will recall that life did not go well for Sara. In the middle of her birthday party, word reaches the school that her beloved Papa has died. His fortune has been confiscated and she is penniless. With no means to pay for her private education, Sara is demeaned, put to work, treated cruelly, and sent to live in the barren attic.

But the love Sara's father poured into her heart has made a lasting impact. Poor, bereft, and ill-treated, Sara has a heart of gold. She says to herself, "Whatever comes, cannot alter one thing. *If I am a princess in rags and tatters,*

I can be a princess inside. It would be easy to be a princess if I were dressed in a cloth of gold, but it is a great deal more of a triumph to be one all the time when no one knows it" *(The Little Princess)*.

You can know it. You can know you're a beloved daughter of the King.

But you must take your Question to God. Remember, you still have a question in your heart. *It's time to ask your True Father, "Am I lovely? Do you delight in me? Am I a captivating woman?"* Wait for him to answer. He will. Not with the voice of disappointment or condemnation. "For there is no condemnation for those who are in Christ Jesus" (Romans 8:1). Maybe it would help to begin with this thought: What if the world has been wrong about you? They were wrong about Cinderella and Snow White. What if the message given to you through your wounds simply isn't true about you? Let that sink in. It wasn't true. *What does this realization free you to do?* Weep? Rejoice? Let go? Reclaim your heart?

Let God speak to you what is true. *Take the risk of faith.* In fact, what he will say is so close to what you have been longing for all these years you'll think you are making it up. That it's too good to be true. But can we out-dream the goodness of God? Can we be more generous than he is? *God wants you to know how much he delights in you.* Today. Every day. Perhaps the answer will come to you through a favorite song on the radio. Or the resurfacing of a cherished memory. Or from a familiar passage of scripture that seems to leap off of the page! He will answer you.

Keep asking him, Father, how do you see me as a woman?

CHAPTER FOUR

WHO IS THIS *Prince*?

*I*n the fairy tales we first loved as little girls, the Prince comes to rescue the Beauty with strength and passion. He is strong. He is brave. He is relentless. *Nothing will dissuade the Prince from freeing his Love.* In full battle regalia, the Prince in *Sleeping Beauty* slashes through the tangled, dangerous thorns that surround the castle and keep Briar Rose in captivity. In *Cinderella*, the Prince scours the countryside determined to find his one true love. In *Snow White*, the Prince rides his horse to discover the princess, kiss her awake, and take her away to the castle of her dreams.

Princes are noble. Princes are brave. They go on quests to save people. They are faithful and true. They are strong, kind, gentle, and handsome. All these Princes are archetypes, metaphors, pictures of *Someone who embodies all the qualities we consider noble and worthy*. And not only do we get a glimpse of this Someone in fairy tales, but in other stories as well.

In the film *Titanic*, Jack sacrifices his life to save Rose. She says of him, "He saved me in every way a woman can be saved." In *Braveheart*, William Wallace gives up his life without saying a word, save one: "Freedom." He dies with his gaze fixed on his beloved, true to the end in his purpose to bring freedom to his people. In *Gladiator*, Maximus fights the evil emperor with the sole purpose of bringing freedom to the people and realizing the dream of a noble country. "Free the prisoners," commands the guard at Maximus's command. And can we forget the words of his friend at the end of the film? His friend looks up to the sky to thank the dead hero, saying, "Now we are free. And I will see you again. But not yet. Not yet."

Princes are willing to die for the ones they love.

The Bible tells us in Revelation that the writer "saw heaven standing open and there before me was a white horse, whose rider is called Faithful and True. With justice he judges and makes war. His eyes are like blazing fire and on his head are many crowns" (19:11-12). He comes riding a white horse with fire in his eyes and a sword in his hand? Whoa! *Who is this Prince we love and long for?* Who is this one endowed with such nobility, integrity, and strength? Who is this that will give his very life to save the ones he loves?

His name is Jesus. He has come for us. *Jesus is, was, and ever shall be, our true Prince, our Knight in shining armor, our Hero.* You can know him like this. Really.

Made for Romance

In the previous chapter, I said that knowing God as Father is beautiful and vital and that our passage into womanhood needs to involve a deep experience of his love. In fact, we will return here over time for healing, because there are young places in our hearts that need to know this still. We will never abandon this part of our relationship with God. But Jesus is calling us to more. *We are to become whole, mature women who know God also as Lover.*

Indeed, if we will listen, a Sacred Romance calls to us through our heart every moment of our lives. It whispers to us on the wind, invites us through the laughter of good friends, reaches out to us through the touch of someone we love. We've heard it in our favorite music, sensed it at the birth of our first child, been drawn to it while watching the shimmer of a sunset on the ocean. The Romance is even present in times of great personal suffering; the illness of a child, the loss of a marriage, the death of a friend. Something calls to us through experiences like these and rouses an inconsolable longing deep within our heart, wakening in us a yearning for intimacy, beauty and adventure.

This longing is the most powerful part of any human personality. It fuels our search for meaning, for wholeness, for a sense of being truly alive. However we may describe this deep desire, it is the most important thing about us, our heart of hearts, the passion of our life. And the voice that calls to us in this place is none other than the voice of God.

[THE SACRED ROMANCE]

God has been wooing you ever since you were a little girl. Yes, we said earlier that the story of your life is the story of the long and sustained assault upon your heart by the one who knows what you could be and who therefore fears you. But that is only part of the story. *Every story has a villain. Every story also has a hero.* The Great

Love Story the Scriptures are telling us about also reveal a Lover who longs for you.

The story of your life is also the story of the long and passionate pursuit of your heart by the One who knows you best and loves you most.

God has written the Romance not only on our hearts but all over the world around us.

What we need is for him to open our eyes, to open our ears that we might recognize his voice calling to us, see his hand wooing us in the beauty that quickens our heart.

Longer than there've been fishes in the ocean
Higher than any bird ever flew
Longer than there've been stars up in the heavens
I've been in love with you.

Stronger than any mountain cathedral
Truer than any tree ever grew
Deeper than any forest primeval
I am in love with you.

—DAN FOGLEBERG, *"Longer"*

What romanced your heart as a girl? Horses in a field? The fragrance of the air after a summer rain? Was it a favorite book like *The Secret Garden*? The first snowfall of winter?

Those were all whispers from your Lover, notes sent to awaken your heart's longings. It was he who called to us even through the fairy tales we loved.

And as we journey into a true intimacy with God as women, he often brings those things back into our lives, to remind us he was there, to heal and restore things that were lost or stolen.

Opening Our Hearts to the Romancer

Every song you love, every memory you cherish, every moment that has moved you to holy tears, *all have been given to you from the One who has been pursuing*

you from your first breath in order to win your heart.
God's version of flowers and chocolates and candlelight
dinners comes in the form of sunsets and falling stars,
moonlight on lakes and cricket symphonies, warm wind,
swaying trees, lush gardens, and fierce devotion.

This is immensely personal. *God's romantic gifts will
be specifically for* your *heart.* He knows what takes
your breath away, knows what makes your heart beat
faster. We have missed many of his love notes simply

because we shut down our hearts in order to endure the pain of life. Now, in our healing journey as women, we must open our hearts again and keep them open. Not foolishly, not to anyone and anything. But yes, *we must choose to open our hearts again* so that we might hear his whispers, receive his kisses.

What is it that God wants from us?

God wants the same thing that you want. He wants to be loved. He wants to be known as only lovers can know one another. He wants intimacy with you. Yes, yes, he wants your obedience but only when it flows out of a heart filled with love for him. "All those who love me will do what I say" (JOHN 14:23 NLT). Following hard after Jesus is the natural response of a captured heart that has fallen deeply in love with him.

Reading George MacDonald several years ago I came across an astounding thought. You've probably heard that in every human heart there is a place that God alone can fill. (Lord knows we've tried to fill it with everything else, to our utter dismay). But the old poet was saying that there is also in God's heart a place that you alone can fill. "It follows that there is also a chamber in God himself, into which none can enter but the one, the individual." You. *You are meant to fill a place in the heart of God that no one and nothing else can fill.*

You are the one who overwhelms his heart with just one glance of your eyes (Song of Songs 4:9). You are the one he sings over with delight and longs to dance with across mountaintops and ballroom floors (Zephaniah 3:17). *You are the one who takes his breath away* by your beautiful heart that against all odds hopes in him. Let that be true for a moment. Let it be true of you.

God wants to live this life together with you, to share in your days and decisions, your desires and disappointments. He wants intimacy with you in the midst of the madness and mundane, the meetings and memos, the laundry and lists, the carpools and conversations, and projects and pain. He wants to pour his love into your heart, and he longs to have you pour yours into his. *God wants your deep heart, that center place within that is the truest you.* He is not interested in intimacy with the woman you think you are supposed to be. He wants intimacy with the real you.

The Prince of Peace, the King of all kings, loves us! This love from him is not something we must struggle for, earn, or fear to lose. It is bestowed. He has bestowed it upon us. He has chosen us. *And nothing can separate us from his love* (ROMANS 8:39). *Not even we, ourselves.* We are made for such a love. Our hearts yearn to be loved above and beyond all others. We are created to be the object of desire and affection of one who is totally and completely in love with us.

And we are.

An intimate relationship with Jesus is not only for other women—for women who seem to have their acts together, who appear godly, and who keep their thighs slimmed down. It is for each and every one of us. God wants intimacy with you. In order to have it, you, too, must offer it to him.

Adoring Hearts

> As Jesus and his disciples were on their way, he came to a village where a woman named Martha opened her home to him. She had a sister called Mary, *who sat at the Lord's feet listening to what he said.* But Martha was distracted by all the preparations that had to be made. She came to him and asked, "Lord, don't you care that my sister has left me to do the work by myself? Tell her to help me!"
>
> "Martha, Martha," the Lord answered, "you are worried and upset about many things, but only one thing is needed. Mary has chosen what is better, and it will not be taken away from her."

LUKE 10:38–42, EMPHASIS ADDED

We've all heard the story about Martha and Mary. *Don't be such a Martha. Got it.* But we've often wondered what "one thing" was needed. We've even heard teaching that it was one simple casserole dish, that Martha was busy making a complicated meal when only one simple food was needed. No, that is not what Jesus is saying. Jesus has again spoken straight into the heart of the matter. *The one thing that is needed is a captivated, adoring heart.* A heart that responds to the extravagant love of God with worship.

Our hearts are made to worship. It is what we do; we can't help it. Now, worship is one of those words made sickly by religion. We hear "worship" and we think, *She's talking about going to church. Singing hymns.* Nope. Worship is far more passionate, far more abandoned. *Worship is giving our hearts away in return for a promise of Life.* Some people worship fashion, others football teams. We really are limitless in what we will give our hearts

away to. Movies, food, shopping, gossip, you name it, I've bowed before them all.

But Jesus is the only one worthy of our heart's devotion. Mary recognized who Jesus was: the source of all Life. *Love Incarnate.* She did what you and I hope we, too, would have done. She dropped everything and sat at his feet, fixing both the gaze of her eyes and the gaze of her heart upon him.

Martha here is much like the busy church, a distracted bride. Recently I was having lunch with a longtime friend. Telling me about the church she was involved in, she said it was focused on the Great Commission and obeying the First Commandment, "to love our neighbors as ourselves." I was struck dumb. That is not the First Commandment. Jesus says the first and greatest commandment is "Love the Lord your God with all your heart and with all your soul with all your mind" (Matthew 22:37). Jesus wants us to love one another, yes. He wants us to serve one another, yes. *But first and foremost, Jesus wants our utter devotion and love for him.*

It is from hearts filled with love for him that all good works and acts of love flow.

A woman's worship brings Jesus immense pleasure and a deep ministry. You can minister to the heart of God. You impact Him. You matter. Jesus desires you to pour out your love on him in extravagant worship that ministers to his heart. This is not just for women who have the time, women who are really spiritual. *You are made for romance, and the only one who can offer it to you consistently and deeply is Jesus.*

Offer your heart to him.

Cultivating Intimacy

When I first began to worship Jesus in the privacy of my bedroom, I listened to one song over and over again. It's a simple song made up primarily of the words,

> *Help us, our God.*
> *We come to you desperately needy.*

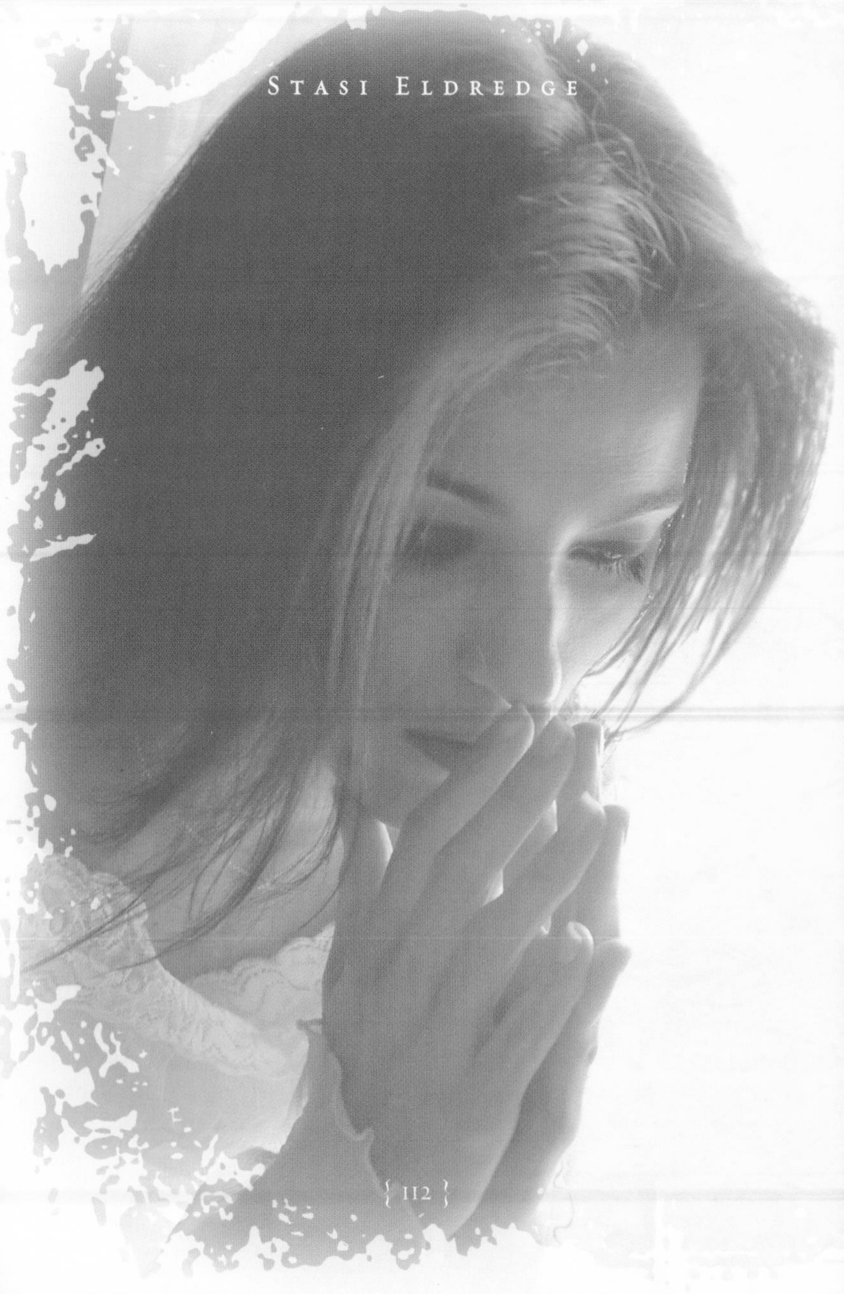

Yes. That is me. I was then (and remain still) desperately needy for God. My struggle with an addiction to food and a deep loneliness were very real. *I needed God to be more tangible, more real in my life.* Filled with a deep hunger for his touch within my heart, thirsty for more revelation of who he truly is, and desperate for deeper healing, I began to set aside several hours each week to devote to private worship. I asked him to come.

I made room for worship in my life's schedule and fought to protect the time. Whether it required unplugging the phone, arranging childcare for my young boys, or staying up after everyone was asleep, it was worth it. *I became captivated by his beauty. It was rich. It was good. And it was* opposed. To pursue intimacy with Christ, you will have to fight for it. You'll need to fight busyness (Martha's addiction). You'll need to fight accusations. You'll need to fight the thief that would steal your Lover's gifts to you outright. That's okay. The fierceness in women was given to us for a purpose. Getting time with your Lover is worth whatever it costs.

Ask his help in making you desperately hungry for him.
Ask his help in creating the time and space you need to draw close to him.
Ask him to come, to reveal himself to you as the Lover that he is.

The Healing of Our Hearts

And now for something really cool. The more we come to know God truly, as he is, the more we come to know ourselves truly, become who he created us to be. *As God reveals his identity to us, he also reveals our identity to us.* He writes the true story of who we are on our hearts.

In his presence he answers our deepest questions: "Do you delight in me? Am I captivating?" Have you asked him yet? Go ahead! Because our God answers with a resounding, "YES!" in a million different ways. As he speaks to our deep hearts and we begin to deeply believe his answer, we grow in having our hearts healed, restored, and freed in the love of God.

The culture of women in the church today is crippled by some pervasive lies: "To be spiritual is to be busy. To be

spiritual is to be disciplined. Duty is what God wants."
The truth is . . . *to be spiritual is to be in a
Romance with God.*

The desire to be romanced lies deep in the heart of every
woman. It is for such that you were made. *And you are
romanced, and ever will be.* Now discover it is true.

CHAPTER FIVE

BETWEEN
ONCE UPON A TIME
AND *Happily*
ever After

Have you ever wondered what happened to Snow White after she rode off with her prince to the castle in the sky? What became of Cinderella after she left the confines of the cellar and became the bride of the prince? The spell over Sleeping Beauty is broken, there is a royal wedding, and then what?

Each woman ruled a kingdom alongside her beloved, that's what.

In Heaven, we will rule and reign with our Prince, our Love, our King. Really.

> *"Come, you who are blessed by my Father; take your inheritance, the kingdom prepared for you since the creation of the world"* (MATTHEW 25:34).

> *"We will also reign with him"* (2 TIMOTHY 2:12).

> *"And they will reign for ever and ever"* (REVELATION 22:5).

This is our destiny. We begin to prepare for it by ruling on this side of Heaven. It is now, here, on the earth that God wants us to bring his Kingdom by ruling as his representatives. Let's come back to Genesis for a moment, for our creation tells us of our purpose in life.

When God creates Eve, he calls her an ezer kenegdo. "It is not good for the man to be alone, I shall make him a [*ezer kenegdo*]" (2:18). Hebrew scholar Robert Alter, who has spent years translating the book of Genesis, says this phrase is "notoriously difficult to translate." The various attempts we have in English tend to be "helper" or

"companion" or the notorious "help meet." Why are these translations so incredibly wimpy, boring, flat . . . disappointing? What is a help meet, anyway? What little girl dances through the house singing "One day I shall be a help meet?" Companion? A dog can be a companion. Helper? Sounds like Hamburger Helper. Alter is getting close when he translates this phrase "sustainer beside him." The word *ezer* is used only twenty other places in the entire Old Testament. And in every other instance *the person being described is God himself,* when you need him to come through for you *desperately.*

There is no one like the God of Jeshurun who rides on the heavens to help you. . . . Blessed are you, O Israel! Who is like you, a people saved by the LORD? He is your shield and helper and your glorious sword.

DEUTERONOMY 33:26, 29

I lift up my eyes to the hills—where does my help come from? My help comes from the LORD, the Maker of heaven and earth.

PSALM 121:1–2

May the LORD answer you when you are in distress; may the name of the God of Jacob protect you. May he send you help.

PSALM 20:1–2

Most of the contexts in the verses above are life and death, by the way, and God is your only hope. Your *ezer*. If he is not there beside you . . . you are dead. A better translation therefore of *ezer* would be "lifesaver." *Kenegdo* means alongside, or opposite to, a counterpart. *You, woman, are called to be a lifesaver, life-giver.* It is written on your heart.

Our Lives

Some of us are called to
the mission field overseas.
Some of us are called to the
marketplace here. Some will be
nurses, doctors, mothers, midwives,
counselors, artists, interior decorators,
engineers, lawyers, poets . . . you name it! But
each one of us is called to become an *ezer*—
a life-offering, lifesaving woman—
who lives in her unique calling and
offers her glory to the world and for
the glory of God. A life that flows out
of our intimacy with Jesus.

You have a role to play.
*You have a high and
holy calling.*

Whether it is holding the hand of kindergarteners as they begin their journeys into school or holding the hands of those dying in hospice care when the veil between worlds is whisper thin, you have a vital role to play. As a woman.

Life is holy. Every moment. God is as present in your car as he is in the sanctuary. He is as busy about his kingdom work in your church as he is in your office. Whether you're in the worship service or in the line at the grocery store, *it all matters.* The mountaintops as well as the mundane. It is in the everyday tasks, the miniscule decisions, the unseen actions and the millions of choices that are ours to make every single day that the Kingdom of God advances or retreats. It all matters.

The world needs you. *Everyone here needs you to awaken to God more fully.* We need you to awaken to the desires of the heart that he placed within you—*so that* you will come alive to him and to the role that is yours to play. Perhaps you are meant to be a concert musician. Perhaps a teacher. Perhaps you are meant to be a neurologist. Perhaps a horse trainer. Perhaps you are to be an activist for the environment or the poor or the aged or the ill. Whatever your particular calling, *you are meant to grace the world with your dance, to follow the lead of Jesus wherever he guides you.* He will lead you first into himself, and from that intimacy he will lead you into the world that he loves and came to save. He needs you. We need you.

Care for Your Heart

For you to live with an awakened heart and play the role that is yours to play, for you to live in intimacy with Jesus, *you must take care of your heart.* Remember Proverbs 4:23?

Above all else, guard your heart, for it is the wellspring of life!

The Bible says guard your heart because it is the wellspring of your life, because *it is a treasure,* because whatever you have to offer in this life flows from that place. How kind of God to give us this warning, like someone entrusting their most precious

possession to a friend and telling them, "Be careful
with this—it means a lot to me."

Above all else? Good grief—we almost never guard our
hearts so carefully. We might as well leave our purse on
the seat of the car with the windows rolled down—we're
that careless with our hearts. "If not for my careless
heart," sang Roy Orbison. The phrase could easily be the
anthem for our lives. Things would be different. I would
be farther along. My faith would be much deeper. My
relationships so much better. My life would be on the
path God meant for me . . . if not for my careless heart.
We live completely backwards; we guard "all else"
above our hearts. For most of us, caring for our hearts
isn't something we even consider.

What Will You Do?

How would you live differently if you believed your heart
was the treasure of the kingdom? You would protect it,
wouldn't you? You would nurture it.

God wants you to. *Your heart matters.*

So—what does your heart need? In some sense this is a personal question, unique to each person's makeup and what brings us life. For some it's music, for others it's friendship. Others need to garden. Some love time in the city while others can't wait to get out of one. Yet there are some things all hearts need in common.

Each of us needs beauty—that's clear enough from the fact that God has filled the world with it, as he has given us sun and rain,

> *Wine that gladdens the heart of man,*
> *Oil to make his face shine,*
> *And bread that sustains his heart.*

PSALM 104:15

Each of us needs silence and solitude—time alone with our heart—and often. Jesus modeled that, although few of us follow his example. Not even one full chapter into the gospel of Mark, there's quite a stir being created by the Nazarene. "The whole town gathered at the door," which is to say that Jesus was becoming the man to see.

Let's pick up the story there:

> That evening after sunset the people brought to Jesus all the sick
> and demon-possessed. The whole town gathered at the door, and
> Jesus healed many who had various diseases. . . . Very early in
> the morning, while it was still dark, Jesus got up, left the house
> and went off to a solitary place, where he prayed. Simon and his
> companions went to look for him, and when they found him,
> they exclaimed: "Everyone is looking for you!" Jesus replied, "Let
> us go somewhere else . . ." (1:35–38).

Everyone is looking for you. Surely you can relate to that.

At work, at home, at church, *aren't there times when
everything seems to come down on you?* Now to be
fair, this is also a tremendous opportunity. I mean, if Jesus
really wants to launch his ministry, increase sales, expand
his audience, this sure looks like the chance to do it. But
what does Jesus do? He leaves. He walks away. This is so
counterintuitive. I mean, strike while the iron's hot, right?
Everyone is looking for you! Oh, really . . . then we'd
better leave. It cracks me up.

Jesus refuses to be ruled by the expectations of others.
Wendell Berry might have been writing of Jesus when

he said, "His wildness was in his refusal—or his inability—to live within other people's expectations." *We are just the opposite;* our entire lives are governed by others' expectations, and when we live like that, our hearts are always the first things to go. Then we wonder why we have nothing left to offer.

And do not forget we are at war. Our enemy has a strategy against every age. The Age of Reason tossed the heart aside, orphaned it like an unwanted child, left it exposed to

the ravages of the Evil One. *The spirit of the age we live in now is* Busyness, *or* Driven. Do I exaggerate? Ask the people you know how things are going. Nine out of ten will answer something to the effect of "really busy."

To counter this, God gives the whole notion of the Sabbath rest. It comes from the creation account in Genesis. For six days God works pretty hard. The phrase that describes him just before he launches into creation, "the spirit of God was hovering over the waters" (1:2) is an active phrase. It's used elsewhere of a mother eagle fluttering over her young, involving as Robert Alter points out, "both nurture as well as rapid back-and-forth movement." But on the seventh day God rested. And he encourages us to do the same, which, by the way, means that *if you are exhausted by your church activities you've missed the point entirely.* "The Sabbath was made for man," said Jesus, not the other way around (**MARK 2:27**).

There is a rhythm to life. Every day we wake, and every night we sleep. The heart beats, then rests. It beats, then rests. For every beat there is a rest. For every hundred beats there are just as many rests. *O, that I would live like this in the rhythm of my heart.* Yes, love and give . . . and then pull away for awhile. By all means, work hard . . . then play. Battle cannot be avoided . . . but let me seize the rest when I can.

And here is a secret. *Women are at their most beautiful when they are* at rest. Not striving. Not grasping. Not fearful. But resting. And we can be at rest, too, at rest in the love of God. Zephaniah assures us, "He will quiet you with his love" (3:17). God is saying, *All is well. It's all going to be alright. I have you. I love you. I will never leave you or abandon you. You are my delight. You are Mine.* In the great heart of God, there is room for us to lie down and rest.

You are romanced. You are the Beauty of the kingdom. And you have an irreplaceable role to play. You are to carry on the invasion by the kingdom of God. And as you know from reading the newspaper and walking out your front door, we are not living in a peaceful kingdom. Rather, *we were born into a world at war.*

To have the life that Jesus invites us into and wants us to have requires something of us every single day and in many moments throughout each day. We have to choose him. Return our hearts to him. *We have to answer his invitation.*

The Invitation

The story of Cinderella turns upon an invitation.

Until the moment when the courier from the palace arrives, Cinderella's life seems set in stone. She will always be a washerwoman, a cellar girl. Her enemies will forever have the upper hand. She will suffer nobly through a life of disappointment. No better life seems possible. This is

her fate. Then, word from the Prince arrives, an invitation to a ball. It is at that point all hell breaks loose. *Cinderella's longings are awakened.* Her enemies become enraged. And her life is never the same.

How gracious that life-change comes by invitation. As a woman, you don't need to strive or arrange or make it happen. You only need to respond. Granted—Cinderella's response took her into a major battle; it took courage to go forth and steadfastness to hang in there through her fears even after she danced with the Prince. It is a beautiful parable of our story.

The same holds true, though in far weightier a manner, for Mary, the mother of Jesus. Her life also turned upon an invitation. The angel came as the courier of the King. But still, she needed to say yes. God would not force her to play so great a role in his plan. Her heart needed to be willing.

She would need her heart through all that followed.
It required remarkable courage, and all hell broke loose
as well. Her Enemy raged. She nearly lost her marriage.
She and Joseph certainly lost their standing
in the synagogue. Mary
needed a steadfastness of
heart to keep saying
yes after the angel
first came.

The invitations of our Prince come to us in all sorts of ways. He seems to work with men largely in the form of challenge—arranging events that require them to rise up as men. But he seems to come to women in the forms of invitation. Because you're a woman, your heart itself is an invitation. An invitation delivered in the most intimate and personalized way. *Your Lover has written something on your heart.* It is a call to find a life of romance and protect that love affair as your most precious treasure. A call to cultivate the beauty you hold inside and unveil your beauty on behalf of others. And it is a call to be the *ezer* the world desperately needs you to be.

Jesus, the true Prince, is inviting you.
He awaits your response.

Will you say yes?

My Lover spoke and said to me,

"Arise, my darling,

My beautiful one,

and come with Me."

SONG OF SONGS 2:10

ABOUT THE AUTHOR

Stasi Eldredge is the coleader of the women's ministry of Ransomed Heart™ Ministries in Colorado Springs, Colorado, where she is passionate about women discovering their identity as the Beloved of Christ. Stasi is drawn to the beauty of the West and would more likely be found outside adventuring than inside tending her home. She loves her family—her husband, John, and their sons, Samuel, Blaine, and Luke—bubble baths, deep conversations, the wind, a dog named Scout, someone else doing the dishes, a good movie, a good cry, a horse named Cora, and "most of all, how God loves me and surprises me by continuing to come for my heart in amazing and intimate ways."

To learn more about John and Stasi's ministry,
visit www.ransomedheart.com.

CONTINUING THE JOURNEY

Captivating. If *Your Captivating Heart* whets your appetite for understanding the beautiful ways God loves his daughters, *Captivating*, by John and Stasi Eldredge, will provide you with a full meal to savor and digest.

BOOKS BY JOHN ELDREDGE

The Way of the Wild Heart
The Ransomed Heart
Epic
Waking the Dead
Wild at Heart
The Journey of Desire
The Sacred Romance (coauthored with Brent Curtis)